Disclaimer:

This work may not be copied, sold, used as content in any manner or your name put on it until you buy sufficient rights to sell it or distribute it as your own from us and the authorized reseller/distributer.

Every effort has been made to be accurate in this publication. The publisher does not assume any responsibility for errors, omissions or contrary interpretation. We do our best to provide the best information on the subject, but just reading it does not guarantee success. You will need to apply every step of the process in order to get the results you are looking for.

This publication is not intended for use as a source of any legal, medical or accounting advice. The information contained in this guide may be subject to laws in the United States and other jurisdictions. We suggest carefully reading the necessary terms of the services/products used before applying it to any activity which is, or may be, regulated. We do not assume any responsibility for what you choose to do with this information. Use your own judgment.

Any perceived slight of specific people or organizations, and any resemblance to characters living, dead or otherwise, real or fictitious, is purely unintentional.

Some examples of past results are used in this publication; they are intended to be for example purposes only and do not guarantee you will get the same results. Your results may differ from ours. Your results from the use of this information will depend on you, your skills and effort, and other different unpredictable factors.

It is important for you to clearly understand that all marketing activities carry the possibility of loss of investment for testing purposes. Use this information wisely and at your own risk.

Access my exclusive Viral Marketing Video Training 2018 at viral.cundell.com/upgrade!

Table of Contents

Introduction   03

Section 1: Viral Marketing Basics
- Chapter 1: What Is Online Marketing All About?   06
- Chapter 2: What is Viral Marketing?   08
- Chapter 3: How Can Viral Marketing Help Your Business?   10
- Chapter 4: Shocking Viral Marketing Facts To Consider   12

Section 2: Viral Marketing – Step by Step
- Chapter 5: The Anatomy Of Viral Marketing Content   15
- Chapter 6: The Best Ways To Deliver Viral Marketing Content   18
- Chapter 7: Where To Find The Right Audience For Going Viral   21
- Chapter 8: Getting Started With A Viral Website   24
- Chapter 9: Getting Viral Marketing Ideas Before Creating Content   28
- Chapter 10: Creating A Profitable Viral Post   31

Section 3: Advanced Viral Marketing Strategies
- Chapter 11: Going Viral With Video   34
- Chapter 12: Going Viral On Social Media   36
- Chapter 13: Using StumbleUpon To Go Viral Easily   38
- Chapter 14: Going Wildly Viral With Email Contests   40
- Chapter 15: Crazy Secret Viral Marketing Tactics That Work   43
- Chapter 16: Optimizing Your Viral Marketing Campaigns   46

Section 4: Additional Tips to consider
- Chapter 17: Do's and Don'ts   50
- Chapter 18: Premium tools and Services to consider   54
- Chapter 19: Shocking Case Studies   57
- Chapter 20: Frequently Asked Questions   67

Conclusion   71

Top Resources   72

Introduction:

Welcome to the latest and very easy to apply "Viral Marketing Made Easy 2018" Training, designed to take you by the hand and walk you through the process of getting the most out of Viral Marketing, for your business.

I'm very excited to have you here, and I know that this will be very helpful for you.

This exclusive training will show you step-by-step, topic by topic, and tool by tool, what you need to know to dominate Viral Marketing, in the easiest way possible, using the most effective tools and in the shortest time ever.

This training is comprised of 20 chapters organized into 4 sections. This is exactly what you are going to learn:

Section 1: Viral Marketing Basics

In Chapters 1 through 4, we'll talk about:

- ✓ What Is Online Marketing All About?
- ✓ What is Viral Marketing?
- ✓ How Can Viral Marketing Help Your Business?
- ✓ Shocking Viral Marketing Facts To Consider

Section 2: Viral Marketing – Step by Step

In Chapters 5 through 10, we'll talk about:

- ✓ The Anatomy Of Viral Marketing Content
- ✓ The Best Ways To Deliver Viral Marketing Content
- ✓ Where To Find The Right Audience For Going Viral
- ✓ Getting Started With A Viral Website

Access my exclusive Viral Marketing Video Training 2018 at viral.cundell.com/upgrade!

- ✓ Getting Viral Marketing Ideas Before Creating Content
- ✓ Creating A Profitable Viral Post

Section 3: Advanced Viral Marketing Strategies

In Chapters 11 through 16, we'll talk about:

- ✓ Going Viral With Video
- ✓ Going Viral On Social Media
- ✓ Using StumbleUpon To Go Viral Easily
- ✓ Going Wildly Viral With Email Contests
- ✓ Crazy Secret Viral Marketing Tactics That Work
- ✓ Optimizing Your Viral Marketing Campaigns

Section 4: Additional Tips to consider

In Chapters 17 through 20, we'll talk about:

- ✓ Do's and Don'ts
- ✓ Premium tools and Services to consider
- ✓ Shocking Case Studies
- ✓ Frequently Asked Questions

Well, it's time for you to start getting the most out of Viral Marketing, on behalf of your Business. I know you'll love this training.

Paul Cundell

Viral Marketing
Made Easy 2018

Section 1
Viral Marketing Basics

Access my exclusive Viral Marketing Video Training 2018 at viral.cundell.com/upgrade!

Chapter 1: What Is Online Marketing All About?

We are all familiar with the word "marketing", and we all have a pretty good idea of what marketing is all about: building a strong brand presence by spreading a brand-centric message. Yet we often fail to properly identify what marketing is all about, thinking of it as nothing but paid advertising, which is actually just one of the many ways that there are of driving a marketing message.

To illustrate this point, we can all recognize a brand-sponsored billboard on a busy venue as advertising, and can rightfully categorize it as marketing, yet we would mostly fail to identify a brand-centric conversation between random people on the streets as marketing.

This is important to understand because a marketer needs to identify every possible way of driving brand-centric conversations outside of traditional advertising channels. In that sense, marketing NEEDS to feel natural.

And make no doubt, it is the same on the internet. Online marketing can be strictly conceptualized as the process of promoting a business, a brand, a product, or a service all over the internet using the right type of marketing strategies and tools that can drive online-specific objectives such as increasing traffic, capturing leads and getting more sales.

Yet online marketing is a very broad term that encompasses a wide range of online marketing tactics and strategies; That is, every possible activity that can help a marketer achieve a business objective online can be considered as "doing online marketing".

More so, the term "online marketing" is nowadays used interchangeably with the term "content marketing", which is defined as an online marketing approach focused on distributing value through content. Coincidentally, an online marketing campaign that does not deliver valuable content is simply doomed to fail from the get go, hence the interchangeable nature of conceptualizations that currently describe the same process.

This groundbreaking shift in priorities has changed the way online marketing is done nowadays, with newer online marketing strategies taking the spotlight alongside classics such as email marketing and banner ads. Examples include:

Search Engine Optimization

Or the process of refining online content in a way that makes it rank higher in search engine results when potential customers use search terms that match keywords in said content.

Social Media Marketing

Using social media platforms such as Facebook, Twitter, and Pinterest to drive organic brand-centric conversations has become a must in this socially-connected modern day internet.

Video Marketing

Online video is now more popular than TV, and there are thousands of businesses making lots of money by using video sharing platforms to promote their products.

These new developments are great and all, but what if you can give them a little edge? What if you could take them to the next level? What if you can go, let's say… viral? Follow our next chapter to learn more!

Chapter 2: What is Viral Marketing?

Hey there my friends! As you might know now, marketing is all about spreading the word about a brand, a business, a product, or a service, using the right type of strategies and resources across channels more likely to be effective when it comes to reaching the right audience with our marketing message.

Online marketing is just like that as well, with the added emphasis on delivering valuable content to the right audience at the right time. Now, there is one seemingly innocuous characteristic of online marketing that gives it an immense advantage compared to offline marketing: reach.

Offline marketing's reach is no match to online marketing's, which has the advantage in all fronts, from costs to available marketing channels, to demographic reach and timing.

Online marketing can easily reach a lot more people across many geographical locations at a faster rate and at a much lower cost when compared to offline marketing. Besides, online marketing has another trick up its sleeve: it can go viral.

Now, all of us are also familiar with the phrase "going viral", and we can mostly agree on what "going viral" means on a very superficial level. That is, that "going viral" means to spread really fast and to reach a lot of people in a very short time.

But "going viral" is not something that is specific to marketing. In fact, "going viral" is something that occurs by accident or luck most of the time, as there is no certainty as to whether something will go viral when it first appears.

That is because a piece of content will go viral if enough people are enticed it to share it virally. Examples of things going viral are ample. Memes, videos, songs and even pictures go viral out of sheer coincidence just because they hit an emotional button that makes people want to share them with everybody they know.

And Then There Is Viral Marketing

Viral marketing is simply marketing that is designed to spread virally. Simply put, it is marketing that is created to "go viral", and it is defined by the following criteria:

- ✓ Viral marketing is designed to generate interest in a brand, business, product or service.

- ✓ The goal of a viral marketing campaign is to drive results from generating awareness about what it promotes. It isn't considered viral marketing if it eventually doesn't generate business-centric results such as increased traffic, more leads or sales.

- ✓ Viral marketing doesn't happen by accident or luck. In fact, all viral marketing content spreads because there is a well-designed viral marketing campaign to back it up.

Viral marketing campaigns follow the same structure of common online marketing campaigns while adding a "viral" element to them with the intention of incentivizing targets to share the promoted content.

Which means that viral marketing campaigns are mostly target-driven: the buzz around viral marketing campaigns is created by target interest. That is, the more the target audience shares it, the more successful a viral marketing campaign is.

Viral marketing campaigns are simple to build and execute because you will only need to create an engaging piece of content such as a video, to set off a starting point and then to redirect it to the appropriate channels. One basic template of how a viral marketing campaign works is a viral video that spreads from YouTube to social media and then to instant messaging apps, and so on.

But fast audience response and a wildly wide reach are not the only benefits of viral marketing. Do you want to know how else viral marketing can help your business? Read our following chapter to learn more!

Chapter 3: How Can Viral Marketing Help Your Business?

The benefits of a well-crafted, properly executed online marketing campaign that doesn't limit itself to a single set of banner ads on a single advertising platform can't be underestimated. A marketing campaign that reaches its targets across all possible channels has a greater chance of generating more awareness, more steady traffic and long-term sales cycles.

Now, when you boost a marketing campaign by adding viral elements to it and you succeed in making it go viral, there are additional benefits beyond allowing your business to create an emotional connection with its potential client base. Here are the most relevant ways in which viral marketing can help your business.

It Helps To Build Your Brand

Viral marketing is one of the most powerful ways to drive brand awareness among members of your target audience and even on people outside of it because it's the people themselves who will be promoting your stuff for you if you do the first steps of your viral marketing campaigns right.

The good news is that brand awareness generated through viral marketing creates a very long-lasting impression and greater brand recall because it is generated through the emotional reward of sharing and through sheer repetition of your marketing message across your target channels and beyond.

It Helps You To Better Understand Your Audience

Your first few viral marketing campaigns will become one of your greatest sources of audience data because they will allow you to understand what it is that your audience wants and what they care about; knowledge that you can use to know exactly what type of content you should create in order to stir people's emotions.

Remember, people are more likely to share content that is related to their innermost interests, and viral marketing is fueled by people's inclination to share what they like!

It helps You Grow Your Customer List

A well-executed viral marketing campaign will allow your business to better connect with qualified clients if you follow up with them after engaging them.

The word-of-mouth effect from your campaigns will in turn encourage them to share your content with others the next time that you share it, increasing your chances of growing your customer list through referral channels.

It Provides Your Business Short Bursts Of Quick, Incremental Growth

The "viral" nature of viral marketing will allow you to drive more traffic and quick conversions with each new campaign, which means that your business will grow by small percentages as well by retaining momentum from these campaigns.

It Converts Your Business Into An Authority

Viral Marketing can transform your business into an online authority in your niche thanks to the power of social proof.

That is, the more people that share and discuss your content in a positive way, the more of an authority your business will be perceived as being.

It Lowers Your Marketing Costs In The Long Run

Viral marketing will allow you to cut a significant amount of your marketing costs once you have a large enough following virally sharing your content, which means that your audience will be doing the marketing for you!

Do you want to learn more about why viral marketing is still as hot today as it has ever been? Check out our next chapter to find out!

Chapter 4: Shocking Viral Marketing

Facts To Consider

- ✓ Successful viral marketing campaigns generate over 1 million impressions in short amounts of time, with some campaigns generating from 10 to 100 times more impressions. ([Source](#))

- ✓ So far one of the most widely used ways to generate traffic with viral marketing is to capitalize on controversial topics, as that is the easiest way to spark online conversations and getting people to take sides in the discussion.

    Controversy leads to compulsive sharing not because of cheap shock value but because it subtly offers a differing point or new angle to a topic that deserves discussion. Adding a little controversy to content makes it very, very likely to go viral by triggering extreme emotional responses on the target audience.
    This tactic might sound a little controversial in itself, but bear in mind that only campaigns that have used controversy in a positive way have gone wildly viral, such as Kleenex's "Unlikely Best Friends" campaign. ([Source](#))

- ✓ In order for a marketing campaign to go viral, its content needs to elicit the following emotional responses: Awe, Surprise, Joy, Pride, Hope, Courage, or Humor. ([Source](#))

- ✓ Engagement generated from viral content is used by the Google algorithm as signals to increase a site's search ranking.

    Metrics such as number of relevant authoritative links and social engagement generated from viral marketing campaigns have been seen to increase site visits as much as 750%! ([Source](#))

- ✓ There is such a thing as a "Viral Coefficient", which describes how likely a viral marketing campaign is to break through the noise and go viral. Viral coefficient can be understood as the number of new targets reached generated by one target, or the total number of new leads or impressions referred by each lead that is reached by the campaign.

Going viral successfully is the result of having a viral coefficient above 1, or of generating 1 or more leads or impressions per each target reached with the campaign. If the viral coefficient is below 1, it means that viral sharing is diminishing and that the viral campaign needs to be optimized. (Source)

- ✓ Of all social media platforms, Instagram is driving the largest number of marketing content going viral, with 49% of photos and 60% of videos on the platform reaching over 250 interactions! In contrast, Facebook posts have a hard time reaching Page fans, with only 6% of them seeing potentially viral page promoted content. (Source)

- ✓ Contrary to popular belief, long-form content gets way more shares than short-form content, with content that is 3,000 to 10,000 words long getting over 1,000 more shares than shorter content. (Source)

- ✓ Marketing content with images is twice as likely to go viral than content without images, with over twice the people sharing image-rich content when compared with content with no visuals. (Source)

- ✓ Having an influencer sharing your marketing content can easily multiply the number of times it is shared, thus increasing its chances to go viral. The good news is that you don't have to convince Oprah or any other high-caliber celebrity to share your campaigns; It will be enough to reach a person who is able to multiply shares by at least two for every person he or she reaches! (Source)

Viral Marketing
Made Easy 2018

Section 2
Viral Marketing – Step by Step

Access my exclusive Viral Marketing Video Training 2018 at viral.cundell.com/upgrade!

Chapter 5: The Anatomy Of Viral Marketing Content

So, what does a piece of viral content actually look like? This is a question that deserves a detailed answer because as you might have heard from us beforehand, viral marketing campaigns don't go viral by accident. The way they go viral can be best described as the result of a combination of content-bound elements that encourage campaign targets to forward them virally, and in this chapter we are going to show you what these elements are with a few examples.

Titles That Trigger A Sensation Of Immediacy Or Of Missing Out

The secret behind making someone want to click through a piece of content based on its title text without going full-on click-baiting is to add curiosity inducing keywords and phrases to it.

And to increase the chances of making said content to go viral is to phrase titles in a way that implies scarcity or that hints to the idea that the campaign target is missing out on something that has been kept secret to him or her, or that is just becoming public knowledge right at that moment.

The negative phrasing includes statements such as "you won't believe", "you should stop", "you should avoid", and "things you didn't know", among many other combinations.

Our example of choice is this post which has been titled "30 things you should stop doing to yourself". It has been shared over 670,000 times on Facebook alone, and that is because its title alone ignites curiosity by telling people that there are 30 things that they should stop doing that they might have not been aware of up until that point, which subtly forces them to immediately click and then to share because they would want to spread the satisfactory nature of the content they just checked.

Numbered Titles And List-Based Content

Have you noticed a trend among popular sites that promote other site's content? And that these pieces of promoted content generate ad revenue by going wildly popular? Well, that is no coincidence. They are designed to go viral, and you might have noticed that the most popular viral articles have the following things in common:

- ✓ The titles include a numbered item
- ✓ The articles inside are list articles

Starting in the early 2000s, some websites noticed that their traffic exploded once they started experimenting with list articles, which consists of long-form content divided into smaller, numbered chunks that make it easier for people to read through.

Websites then realized that all they needed to go viral even for short periods of time was to create list-based articles with titles that teased readers to click through. If you are a marketer, you might also recognize that this same formula works when setting up sales pages and lead magnets!

Cracked.com is a great example of this. It generates over 300 million views a month by updating the site daily with list articles. And as you can see just by hanging around the site, most article titles follow a simple formula: Numbered items, niche or trending keywords, and negative phrasing.

Content That Is Easy To Consume And Skim Through

Do you know why scientific abstracts and papers have never gone viral in like, ever? Well, the reason why is because they're just not easy to read, and they don't offer an immediate reward. What you will usually see going viral more often though is content that is easy to read and, most importantly, content that you don't need to digest completely to enjoy it.

In other words, content that you don't have to read in full the first time you click through it and that in fact offers enough value in its simplicity as to be worth a second or third read. That right there is the real marker of a piece of viral content with evergreen potential.

Going back to the viral post that we showed you earlier, the one titled "30 things you should stop doing to yourself", you can see how easy it is for you to simply skim through the sub titles while being able to understand what it's all about, and why the information might be worth sharing with others, who will then replicate your behavior.

Why is that? Because people might enjoy reading the headline, the first paragraph and then skim through all the way to the end of the article, which you can benefit from by placing your affiliate links, sale page links or sign up forms in the middle and at the end of your viral posts.

Sharing Buttons

Share buttons are a must. Content that integrates share buttons is 7 times more likely to spread virally. The easier it is to share the content, the better, as you can see on [this website](), which places share buttons on the lower bar and right above the user's taskbar.

This makes it easier for anyone to share this content at any moment while reading through, and not just once the content ends, which is a missed opportunity because a lot of people won't read through the content in its entirety the first time, and they will be less likely to share it once they go back to finish consuming the content.

Video Repurposing

All of the previously discussed attributes can be repurposed on video format. That is, you can repurpose those same strategies to create viral video marketing campaigns, such as this "[6 reasons to go Pixel 2 over the iPhone X]()" affiliate marketing video campaign, which has generated over 1 million views by applying the exact same formula as list-based content, easy to digest yet smart, informative content, and numbered title.

Now that you know what are the ingredients that make content more likely to go viral, it is time for you to learn what are the best ways to deliver viral content for marketing and business purposes. See you in our next chapter!

Chapter 6: The Best Ways To Deliver Viral Marketing Content

Hey there my good friends! In our previous chapter we showed you what the elements are that make content go viral. Whether isolated or in combination, such elements play a role in helping a marketing campaign to go viral as well as when applied to the contents that make up the actual campaign.

But what about delivery? There's no doubt that delivery plays a role and is as important as the marketing content itself, and in this chapter we are going to tell you all about the best ways to deliver your online viral marketing campaigns no matter what audience you plan to target.

Viral Posts

Most viral marketing campaigns start in the form of a website post. There is a number of reasons for this, but for marketers, the number one reason is because making a viral website or blog post to rank high in search engines is one of the best ways of creating organic relevance for a product or brand when it is just being launched.

Viral website posts are also a great way of making sure that your viral marketing message gets as much visibility and traction as possible because they are easily shareable and can include text, images, videos and interactive media, as long as every element in the post is relevant to the brand or business being promoted.

Viral Videos

Video is also a great format for delivering awesome viral marketing campaigns and, in fact, lots of brands use video as a way of revamping their influence and of raising awareness among the youngest members of their target audience.

One of the greatest advantages of using video as a viral marketing format is that it allows marketers to deliver their marketing message in a visually striking way that engages targets with sight and sound. And once a viral marketing video spreads, there is no stopping it until it reaches peak engagement!

Viral Emails

Email is still one of the most effective marketing channels around, even after all these years of mobile and social media developments. The effectiveness of viral email marketing can be attributed to how email campaigns allow marketers to leverage people's networks to forward their marketing message.

What's also great about viral email marketing is that it can be used to spread any type of viral marketing campaign by using email as a vehicle. For example, you can create a viral marketing campaign that consists of an email that links to a viral blog post that links to a viral marketing video!

Viral Social Media Marketing

Social media has become one of the most significant drivers of viral content since its very inception because they are all about sharing, and marketers have taken advantage of this fact in the smartest ways possible, even coining the "social media marketing" term to describe the use of social media platforms to launch and spread marketing campaigns.

Social media can be used as a channel to spread any type of viral marketing campaigns no matter the format because basically all social media platforms, especially Facebook and Twitter, are designed to allow users to easily share whatever content reaches their timelines.

Whether it is a viral marketing video, a link to a viral marketing website, or a link to a viral email marketing campaign's signup form, people only have to click on a simple "share" button after reacting to a piece of viral marketing content without a second thought, which helps the campaign to have a very wide reach and impact.

Alternate Reality Games

An "Alternate Reality Game" is a network-based type of viral marketing narrative that extends to the real world. Alternate reality games are often used to deliver online viral marketing campaigns, and their role is to seed a campaign by igniting an online invitational campaign to encourage people to participate.

The intention of seeding a viral marketing campaign this way is to get as many people to join the game through viral marketing vehicles such as email invitation forwards and social media tagging. Once the campaign starts, people are given instructions to complete activities in the real world.

These activities are designed to unravel a narrative around a product or service. The difference between this strategy and non-interactive viral marketing is that it involves people participating in the marketing narrative.

The goal of alternate reality games is to spark conversations around a product or service, and they are a very effective viral marketing vehicle because they involve multiple platforms at the same time, and also because they permeate people's daily lives to the point that daily interactions become an opportunity to recruit new players who will keep spreading the marketing message.

Ok, so now that you know what the most efficient viral marketing formats are, where can you find the audience most likely to react to them? We're glad that you asked, because we're about to talk about it in our next chapter. So tune in!

Chapter 7: Where To Find The Right Audience For Going Viral

Hey there my friends! So now that you've got yourself a good viral marketing campaign idea you might be eager to set it up, but how do you know in advance IF your viral marketing idea will actually work, and who is more likely to react to it in a way that helps you go viral? Wonder no more, because here's our list of the top places to find the right audiences for going viral!

Google

You can use Google as a source of audience for your viral campaigns by collecting information about how people talk about your products.

In our example, we are planning to go viral in the health care niche, specifically we are going to target the "diabetes" niche keyword to promote our "diabetes care made easy" business, and we do so by entering our target keyword in Google.

That way, as you can see here we are able to retrieve all kinds of trending information about the niche audience we are going to target to help us make our marketing campaign go viral. Not only that, but we can use long tail keywords to find specific communities that are actively discussing our niche.

Facebook

You can use Facebook to find a qualified audience by entering your niche keyword in the Facebook search bar. Now use the tabs above to collect information. We recommend you to use the "people", "pages", and "groups" tabs to find active Facebook communities that you can target, and to use the "posts", "photos", "videos", and "events" tabs to find the most recent conversations around your target topic.

Once you have used the search function to collect information we recommend you to create a Facebook page from where to launch your campaign if you don't have one.

Use this page to create posts and content that can attract people organically, and secondly to promote these posts and content using the "Facebook ads manager", which you can locate by clicking on the "create ads" option in the profile menu.

Remember to use the information that you collect to target users by pages liked, by groups joined, and by interests.

Twitter

Twitter is also a great platform to make your campaigns go viral. You will simply have to enter your niche keyword in the search bar. Now in the "top" results you will find the posts and accounts that are top-of-mind at the moment of your research.

Look for those tweets with the largest number of retweets and likes, take note of what they are posting about and follow the links and videos on those tweets.

Now simply watch for the accounts posting those tweets and see which ones have the largest number of followers and of follows. Follow those accounts and then look for popular accounts interacting with the tweets posted by those accounts. These account's managers are very likely to follow you back and to retweet your viral campaigns in the future!

YouTube

YouTube is one of the best places to make any content go viral. You can either create a viral video campaign or a video to complement your viral campaign. Use short-form videos that can be watched fast and shared easily. Also, use the information that you collected on Facebook and Twitter to create your video titles, descriptions and tags, as well as trending images for your thumbnails.

Reddit

Reddit is a favorite platform for online marketers because it can help your viral marketing content to gain traction on search engines. Now, don't focus on going viral on reddit. Instead, focus on using reddit as a source of ongoing traffic to your viral campaigns by using the "submit a new link" or "submit a new post" features to share your viral marketing campaigns in a casual way.

Instagram

You can use Instagram to attract organic traffic to your viral campaigns by making a smart use of the search feature to find hashtags that are associated with your niche keyword and how popular they are. You can also check out these hashtags to see the posts that are tagged with these hashtags.

Once you know where to find the people most likely to help you spread your marketing message, you will realize that you will need to have a viral website that you can use to link to your viral marketing campaigns. Ready to set it up? Tune in to our following chapter to teach you how!

Chapter 8: Getting Started With A Viral Website

Hey there my friends! In one of our previous chapters we told you that one of the best ways of delivering viral marketing content is through a viral website. Now, there are certain elements that you need to add to a website to make it help you push viral content out there, and in this chapter we are going to show you how to set up a viral website from scratch, step by step.

The first step is to look for a domain vendor to buy your viral website's domain and a hosting service where to host your viral website, and we recommend you to use "HostGator" as they are our trusted service providers.

To buy your domain name you will simply have to go to "hostgator.com" and click on the "domains" tab. Use the domain name search bar on that page to look for a custom domain name, check its availability and add it to your shopping cart.

Now to buy hosting service simply head back to "hostgator.com" and click on the "web hosting" tab. There you will see three hosting service plans available: the "hatchling plan", the "baby plan" and the "business plan". We recommend you to select the "business plan", as it allows you to install unlimited domains and to easily install WordPress to set up your viral sites!

After you buy your domain name as well as your hosting service plan and register your "cPanel" profile, you will be able to set up your viral website. Start by logging into your cPanel dashboard, look for the "popular links" section and click on "Build a new WordPress site".

Now click on the "select domain for installation" menu, select the domain where you are going to set up your viral website, enter the name of your new viral website or blog in the "directory" field and click on "next".

Now you have to register your new WordPress site's info. Start by entering the name of your new viral site in the "blog title" field.

Enter your admin username in the "admin user" field. This is the user name that you will use to log in to your new viral site. Now enter your "first name" and your "last name".

Lastly, enter your "admin email", check the "terms of service agreement" box, and click on "install". Now wait until you get an "installation complete" message and save your "username" and your "password".

Now click on "login" and on the next page simply enter your username, your password and click on "login" to get inside your new site's dashboard. Now it is time to transform your new WordPress site into an actual viral website!

Start by installing a viral theme on your new website. Go to the "appearance" tab on the left-hand menu and click on the "theme" option. Now scroll down and click on "add a new theme". There are some really good options out there, and we have two recommendations for you. You can choose somewhere in between according to your budget!

To find these themes you will simply have to use the "search themes" search bar. Our first recommendation is the "sociallyviral" theme, which is a premium theme designed to boost social shares, traffic and revenue. It is currently priced at $59, and it is responsive, speed optimized, and SEO ready.

Our second recommendation is the "Hueman" theme, which is a free theme designed to increase your viral traffic and to quickly engage your visitors. It is mobile friendly and fast. We are going to install this theme on our viral website on this example video to show you how to install your viral theme the right way.

Start by clicking on the "install" button corresponding to your theme of choice in the theme search results page. Then click on "activate" once it installs. You will be taken to the "themes" section. Once there click on the "customize" button corresponding to your installed theme.

Initially, you will only need to make minimal customizations to your site. First, click on the "edit" button located to the left of your Blog's name on the header. Start by editing your site's headline in the "tagline" field.

Now go to the "site icon" section and click on the "select image" button. Now click on "select files" and look for your site's logo image inside your computer.

Click on the "select" button once it uploads, and remember to check the "display a logo in the header" option.

Awesome! Now click on the "set your social links" edit button and then click on "add new". This will allow you to add social share buttons that people can use to connect to your social media accounts.

Start by clicking on the "select an icon" menu to select which social media icons you will add. In our example case, we are going to select the "Facebook" icon to add our Facebook page to show you how. Once you select a social icon simply enter your social URL in the "social link url" field and click on "add it".

Awesome! You can do this with as many social pages as you would like to link to, which will help you to increase your chances of going viral.

Later customizations such as "categories" can be done on your own according to your content and your needs, so let's move on to the next step by clicking on the "publish" button to save our changes and then on the "close" button to go back to the dashboard.

The final step to make your WordPress site into a proper viral website is to install viral power plugins on it. To start installing these viral power plugins hover over the "plugins" tab on the left-hand menu and click on "add new".

There are two viral power plugins that will help your viral website to stay top-of-mind, to increase your viral traffic and to increase your revenue. The first one is the "shareaholic" plugin. To install this plugin simply type "shareaholic" on the "search plugins" search bar.

This plugin will allow you to add social sharing buttons to your content, related content recommendations, ad monetization and viral analytics to your site. To install this plugin you will simply have to click on the "install now" button on the plugin, and then to click on "activate".

Lastly, click on the "get started now" button after installing the plugin, and you will be ready to customize the viral options offered by this powerful plugin! Before we proceed, scroll down to the "in-page share buttons" section and check the "above content" option in the "post", "page", and "index" boxes. Now click on "save changes" to continue.

Finally, you will have to install a plugin to allow visitors to post social comments on your viral marketing posts. Once again, hover over the "plugins" tab on the left-hand menu and click on "add new".

Now type "Facebook comments" in the "search plugin" search bar, wait for the results to load, and locate the "Facebook Comments" plugin. Now simply click on the "Install Now" button, then on the "activate" button.

And that's it! Now your website is ready to deliver your viral marketing campaigns. Tune in to our next chapter so we can show you the easiest ways to find inspiration for your viral marketing campaigns!

Chapter 9: Getting Viral Marketing Ideas Before Creating Content

Hey there friends! To make a viral marketing campaign go viral you have to either create an original campaign from scratch or to capitalize on a trending topic that can help boost your campaign.

The thing is that you will never know for sure how viral a piece of content will go, or for that matter if it is ever going to go viral. The good news is that there is so much content going viral online at any given time that you will have to simply take a look around to get fresh ideas that you can reverse-engineer to help your own marketing campaigns and posts to go viral.

In this chapter we are going to show you the easiest way to find inspiration for your next viral content. The key strategy is to browse for trending topics at popular online sources and then to leverage those topics to give a viral boost to your own campaigns.

BuzzFeed Trending

Let's start on "BuzzFeed.com", basically the template for most of all websites that aspire to go viral. As you might already know, BuzzFeed is a website mostly dedicated to tracking online viral content, which already makes it an ideal place to look for inspiration.

Now, what you might not have known is that the BuzzFeed site has a neat feature called "trending", and you can access it by clicking on the "trending" button located on the top bar. As you can see, in this section you will be able to find viral content and trending topics for any niche, and you'll simply have to adapt it to your own posts or campaigns!

BuzzSumo

Now this site will not help you to find trending topics and viral stuff like BuzzFeed does, because it will instead help you to identify what kind of content and conversations have performed well for any specific topic.

This means that you can use it to find the most shared content in your niche. You will simply have to enter your target niche keywords in the "enter topic" search bar and then to click on "go!". Once you get your results you will be able to see how much each piece of content has been shared on the most popular social media platforms, as well as the total number of times it has been shared, with the top performers on top.

YouTube

YouTube is also a great platform to discover what's trending online on any given day. You will simply have to click on YouTube's left-hand menu, and then to click on the "Trending" tab to go to the "trending" videos section, where you will be able to find what's viral among YouTube users.

Reddit

Reddit is one of the best places to discover trending topics because it only aggregates viral content making a lot of noise right at the moment it reaches the site's homepage. The cool thing about reddit is that it will allow you to discover memes, viral macro images, articles or keywords that you can use as quick leverage on your viral website to generate viral traffic organically.

What's Trending

"What's trending" is also an excellent source of trending topics that you can work into your own viral content. It is easy to use and it even shows you content that is trending in real time as well as predictions about content that can go viral at any moment's notice.

HubSpot's Blog Idea Generator

Lastly, there is a tool that you can use once you have found inspiration for your next piece of viral content yet have a hard time getting started. HubSpot's Blog Idea Generator is a browser-based tool that will allow you to use keywords to generate blog post title suggestions.

You will simply have to enter up to three nouns, one on each "noun" field and then to click on the "give me blog ideas!" Button. You will get a list of blog post suggestions that you can use or adapt to your needs!

So now that you know what the elements are to define a piece of viral content and where to find inspiration for your viral posts, it is time for you to learn how to create one for your own viral website's in our next chapter. So tune in!

Chapter 10: Creating A Profitable Viral Post

Hey there everyone! Creating a viral marketing post is easier than you might think, because a viral marketing post is a viral post in which you are going to add an element of monetization, such as a sales page or affiliate link, to name a few, and we are going to show you how to create a viral marketing post on your WordPress site.

Start on your dashboard, hover over the "posts" tab and click on "add new". Let's start with the title. Just like we covered before, numbered titles and teaser titles are the best for increasing viral traffic to your content, so we are going to work a mixture of both types of titles on our own, so we are going to type "5 Diabetes Type 2 Treatments – Number 1 Might Shock You" in the title text area.

Next comes the post images. Start by clicking on the "add media" button. Now, there are two types of media that you can insert in your viral posts. First, insert the "featured image", which will be the image featured on your post's header and right under the title.

Simply click on the "featured image" tab and then either upload the image from your computer or add one from your media library. Once you select your featured image click on "set featured image" to continue.

Now, the second type of viral post image is the images that you will insert into your post, and you will simply have to click on the "add media" button, select the image that you are going to insert on your post and then click on "insert into post".

Let's now compose our viral post content. As you can see here, it is a long-form list article designed to go from the last item on the list all the way to the first. Now, there are two reasons why we teased the first item in our list in the title.

The first reason is because this has the effect of making people curious as to why item Number 1 will shock them as described in the title. And secondly, because we are going to use item Number 1 to promote an affiliate link to a product which offers a solution to the issues outlined in the article.

What we are going to do is to insert the affiliate link where it corresponds, such as where the product is mentioned. Please keep in mind that this is not the only monetization option that you can integrate into your viral posts, and you can perfectly create viral marketing posts to earn ad revenue or increase visits to your online store. The idea is to create a viral post that you can use to drive sales or to generate revenue from your preferred method.

Now before you publish your new viral post make sure to insert tags in the tag section using keywords that you found when you looked for inspiration following the steps outlined in the previous chapters. This will help you to make it easier for your target audience to find and share your viral posts. Now simply click on "publish" and post!

Are you now ready to go several steps above? Well make sure to tune in to our following section so we can teach you how to go viral on social, on video and on email, as well as some advanced-level strategies to increase your viral traffic and conversions. See you there!

Viral Marketing
Made Easy 2018

Section 3

Advanced Viral Marketing Strategies

Access my exclusive Viral Marketing Video Training 2018 at viral.cundell.com/upgrade!

Chapter 11: Going Viral With Video

You might be familiar with online videos going viral all the time, but have you wondered how they do it? How do they reach 2 million views in just 2 days? Granted, most viral video marketing campaigns are backed by huge budgets and big names, but how do brands that are just getting started use video to go viral?

It all starts with having an awesome, entertaining, relevant video where your brand is only featured at the end with an invitation to visit your viral website. Once you have created your video you have to upload it online. Now, some marketers believe that in order to go viral you need to upload your video to as many channels as possible, but it is going to be enough if you upload and seed your viral video on a single platform, and we recommend you to use YouTube.

Start by clicking on the "upload" button while signed in on YouTube, then click on "select files to upload", look for your viral video on your computer, and double click on it to start uploading it. Now you can start entering your viral video's info while you wait for it to upload.

Let's start with the title. Multiple case studies on viral videos that have gotten over 1 million views in less than two days have found the core elements of a viral video title. First, it has to be easy to identify with the audience's perspective, which means that your video title addresses your audience's wants and needs, and secondly, it has to include a strong verb or action phrase to reinforce the positive impact that will make your title resonate.

The last elements are a benefit and the surprise. Your title has to tell your audience why it will be good to check your viral video NOW. So we are going to use this information to create our title with our target audience in mind, so we are going to type "How I Killed My Diabetes WITH FOOD (And How You Can Do It Too!)".

As you can see, we are telling our target audience how we killed our diabetes, which is what they want to know how to do, and we are telling them that we did it with food, which adds an element of surprise and a "wow" factor, and we are telling them how they can do the same, which is the benefit.

Once you create a viral title you won't need to describe your viral video further in the "description" field, but we recommend you to add links to your viral website, your store, your sales pages, and to your social media accounts, as that's what you want to monetize after people watch your viral video. Now add tags to your video. Use only relevant keywords. Lastly, click on "publish" to post your video.

Alright, so once you upload your video you have to actually start marketing your viral video if you want to make it go viral. Start by posting it to Facebook, Twitter, and Reddit, and ask people you trust to share it.

Then look for authoritative blogs in your niche and nicely ask them if they would like to post and discuss your video. For most blogs this will be a great deal as long as your video is good and shareable because it will be a source of traffic for them. Once your video starts getting shared and linked to, it will make it to YouTube's front page.

Want to learn more? Then tune in to our following chapter, where we are going to teach you how to go viral on social media, the easy way!

Chapter 12: Going Viral On Social Media

Hey there my friends! One of the best things about social media platforms is that they are a lot like open chat rooms, where information gets passed over quickly and where truly engaging content has a great chance of going viral.

So how can you easily go viral on social media? You have to start by creating a "social persona", or a social media profile that reflects your target audience. In our case, we have designed the "DCME", which is the social persona that represents our "Diabetes Care Made Easy" business on social media.

As you can see, we have created variations of the same persona with profiles on Facebook, Twitter, and Instagram. This will allow you to find followers that can recognize you as an authority and that can help you to spread your viral content.

Now, you have to learn how to create social media posts that go viral. To go viral on social media you have to follow a series of steps on each one of your social posts, with slight variations on each platform, and we are going to show you the standard viral post layout by creating a viral Facebook post.

First, you will need an engaging piece of visual content, which might be an image or a video. Make sure to always upload images and videos directly to the social platform that you are going to use. In our case, we are going to use the same video we used to go viral on YouTube, so we start by adding it to our post with the "add photo or video" button.

Once your media is uploaded you will have to create the post headline. Because you are going to go viral on social media, go with text that encourages involvement with the post and the content. In our case, we are going to use the "Welcome To The 7 Days Healthy Food Challenge. Are You In?". Adding emojis to your headline make it more visual and engaging, so make sure to add one or two that make sense on your headline.

Then we are going to add a shortened URL to our viral website by going to "bit.ly" in our browser, paste our website's address in the "paste a link to shorten" bar and then click on "shorten". Then we will click on "copy", go back to our post and paste the shortened URL in the headline.

Now we are going to click on "tag friends" to tag people that can help us make this post go viral. Now you'll be ready to publish your viral post, so simply click on "post" to finish.

You will be able to pull this off on other social channels as well but with slight variations. On Twitter and on Instagram for instance you will benefit from adding relevant hashtags to your headlines and from using short form videos.

And that's it! Apply these strategies and you'll soon discover the benefits of using social media to go viral. Next up we will be teaching you how to advertise your content on StumbleUpon to go wildly viral, so make sure to tune in!

Chapter 13: Using StumbleUpon To Go Viral Easily

Hello there my friends! You might already know StumbleUpon as an easy-to-use content discovery engine that can help you boost traffic to your content, but you might not be aware about the platform's paid discovery service.

The StumbleUpon ad service allows publishers and brands to reach the right audience with targeted content distribution. It will help you to make any kind of content with a URL go viral by letting you target your audience by age, gender, location, device and interests.

To start using the service start by going to the "ads.stumbleupon.com" URL in your browser and then clicking either on "get started" to sign up or on "sign in" to log in to your StumbleUpon Ads account.

Once in your account you will simply have to click on "create new campaign". Now you will be asked to enter your promoted URL, a name for your new campaign and a campaign template, both of which are optional.

You will be allowed to insert any type of URL to promote in the "enter URL" field, and in our case, we are going to enter our viral post URL in order to directly funnel viral traffic from StumbleUpon to our viral post, from where it will be easier to monetize our campaign.

Now you will have to "target your audience". You will be able to target people by age, gender, device, location, and interests. In our case, we are going to target people aged "33 to 59", of "all" genders.

We will leave all devices checked, and we will uncheck the "all locations" option to target only English-speaking countries where people are more likely to spend money online.

Now in the "interests" section you will have three different ways to set up your target interests. You can simply type in your interests in the "search interests" bar to add them to your target interests.

Or you can either select "interest bundles" to select your target interests as predefined bundles or "precise targeting" to select your target interests from a list of categories.

In our case, we are going to select "precise targeting", then we are going to select the "health" category, then the "health conditions" sub-category, and then "diabetes" as our target interest within that sub-category. Now we are going to also select the "health solutions" sub-category and then "weight loss" and "health" as our target interests within that sub-category.

Lastly, you will have to "budget" your campaign. Here you will have to enter your daily budget first, and we recommend you to start on a $20 to $25 daily budget. Then you will have to select either to spend your budget "evenly", or "ASAP" if you want to reach people as quickly as possible.

Then you will have to schedule your campaign, and you can simply leave both "start" and "end" fields blank if you don't want to set a schedule. Lastly, you will have to put a price to each "stumble" or person discovering your content, with higher amounts increasing the priority of your ad.

Here we recommend you to check the "engaged visitors only" option to automatically set a proper price that will help you reach engaged targets only.

Once you are ready to launch your campaign you will simply have to click on "submit" and wait for your content to start going viral. And that's it!

Chapter 14: Going Wildly Viral With Email Contests

Hey there my friends! People love free stuff, so it's no surprise that offering a valuable prize in exchange for referring your content is one of the easiest ways to make it go viral. The good news is that it is easy and affordable to do, and we are going to show you how in this chapter!

First, you will need to join "Gleam", an easy-to-use contest marketing platform. You will simply have to go to "gleam.io" on your browser, click on "sign up", and complete the registration process.

Once you sign up you will have to login to be able to create awesome contests the easy way. As you can see, there are several types of contests that you can create, and the one that will help you to get the most viral forwards and shares is the "refer-a-friend" contest.

The "refer-a-friend" contest will allow you to include email actions and viral sharing in your competitions, and you'll need to upgrade your Gleam account to a premium plan in order to set up "refer-a-friend" contests.

So in this chapter we are going to show you how to set up a contest that you can use to promote your viral post on email as well as to encourage subscribers to share it. Start by clicking on the "new competition" button.

First, enter the name of your contest in the "name" field. We recommend you to always use a combination of the name of the prize that you are going to offer and the action required to enter the contest. In our case, we are going to name it "Read On To Win An EasyTouch Test Strips Tri-Pack!".

Now click on the "user details" tab and paste your Facebook Page's URL in the "Allow users to Like a Facebook Page" field. Now click on the "how to enter" tab and select the "visit a page" option.

In the "title" field enter a call-to-action to tell your subscribers to follow on the link. In our case, we are simply going to use the name of the contest here. Now check the "mandatory" and "daily entry" options to increase daily traffic to your viral website.

Now enter your viral post URL in the "link URL" field. Lastly, check the "automatically complete" option to continue. Now click on the "prize" tab and enter the name of your prize in the "name title" field, and enter the number of winners in the "number of winners" field.

Now click on save to finish setting up your contest. On the following page, click on the URL located under "landing page", and then copy that same URL when you're redirected to it.

Now you will simply have to set up an email campaign to forward the contest to your subscribers. In our case, we are going to use "MailChimp", so we start by going to our MailChimp account. Once there we are going to click on "create campaign", and then on the "create an email" option.

Now we are going to name our campaign and click on "begin" to start creating our email. First, we are going to click on "add recipients", then we are going to click on the "choose a list" menu to select our subscriber list.

We are going to send this campaign to all subscribers in our list, so we click on "save" to continue. Now we are going to click on "add subject" to add our subject line. For this campaign we are going to add the name of our "Gleam" contest as our subject line.

We save, and then click on "add from" to add the campaign's sender's name and email address. We save again and then click on "design email". In the "select template" page we are going to click on the "themes" tab to look for a theme that fits our contest, so we select the "competition invitation" theme.

Now what we will simply do is to click on the "edit" buttons corresponding to each block in the design to replace the logo and the image with our brand logo and the image of our prize using the "replace" option.

Now we are going to edit the text in the email to describe our contest. Lastly, we are going to click on the "enter now" button to add our contest URL in the "web address" field. Now we will click on "save and close" to continue.

Now that we are done we will have to "schedule" or "send" this campaign. We want to send it off now, so we simply click on "send", and then on "send now" to forward it immediately to our subscribers. And that's it! You are about to go viral with the power of email contests!

Chapter 15: Crazy Secret Viral Marketing Tactics That Work

Hey there my friends! "Taking shortcuts" gets a bad rep because it is more often than not associated with cheating, but a lot of times "taking a short cut" simply means to apply a highly efficient strategy that will allow you to get faster results. Here are some of the best viral marketing tactics that have allowed us to bypass the hardest steps!

Getting Viral Third-Party Coverage

Getting press mentions and third-party coverage is one of the most precious milestones of online marketing for two reasons. One, because it is difficult to achieve, and second because it significantly increases content exposure.

This strategy, also known as "backlink building", is all about getting popular and authoritative sites, content creators and influencers to share your content. Now, this is not easy to do for a number of reasons.

Authoritative sites and popular content creators are inundated with content sharing requests on a daily basis, so they're very likely to simply ignore them on the basis of surplus connection requests.

What these sites and content creators crave is valuable content that they can publish and share in order to keep their audiences engaged. In that respect, they are after the same type of content that their audiences want, and they are as likely to share it when such content offers them the benefit of being engaging.

Now, there are a lot of marketers that will recommend you to simply create the most awesome and share-worthy content possible and to keep posting it a minimum of three times a week, because that will help you to be eventually discovered and shared by one of these authoritative figures.

And while that is a noble strategy, you will basically be counting on the good fortune of being discovered eventually, at some random point over time. If you want to build back links and get authority status faster, you will need to apply the following steps:

- ✓ Find, collect and list a considerable number of relevant bloggers, columnists, video bloggers and other content creators. Research them and take notes of the type of content that they create. Pay special attention to those who create for bigger online publications, or those who have large followings and important sponsors. Compile their contact details!

- ✓ Create short-form and long-form pieces of newsworthy content that these authority bloggers, sites and content creators can continually share on their own periodical content pieces.

- ✓ Craft individual pieces of personalized email copy to pitch your content based on what you researched about these authority figures and contact them. Keep your email copy short and to the point. Try to add a personalized element based on the type of content the recipient creates or covers on his or her pieces.

- ✓ Keep track of successful conversations and responses. Work on creating a meaningful, professional relationship with the ones that gave you a positive response.

Get Featured On Others Newsletters

Once you have created a professional relationship with these authoritative figures you will need to move on to the next step, which is to be featured in their newsletters, as this will immensely increase your viral reach even when you don't intend to! Remember, this is email we are taking about!

So, how do you go about asking these popular figures to share your content with their email contacts? You have already done the hardest part, which is to make them like your content so much as to make them share it.

Now you will simply have to start by pitching an email-friendly version of your content to them before actually launching it to the public, but you will have to show them that you respect and appreciate their authority status by incentivizing them to email your content; Paying them for the link placement or sharing back their content everywhere you publish your own content are great incentives.

Think Outside The Box

We already mentioned that one of the key ingredients of viral marketing is to add a shocking element of surprise to your marketing material. Using your services or products in an unusual way will help you to achieve this effect.

Take for example "BlendTec", a company that made its products popular thanks to its powerful "Will it blend?" video ad campaign, where they showed their blenders blending the latest products of the time, such as iPhones and video games.

Reward Your Audience

Nothing spreads as virally as a good sweepstake. People love to get free stuff, and you can get lots of exposure by encouraging people to share your content when you tell them that the more they share, the more chances they will get to win your promoted prize!

Take Your Campaign Out In The Wild

This strategy will require you to actually go out and take action on the streets, but it will help you to go viral in ways you didn't know were possible. Now, you don't have to spend a lot of money on this, you will simply have to go somewhere that you know you are likely to find people in your target audience, and once there, you will have to gather a group of people whom to promote your product, website or service through a quick giveaway.

Once you select a winner make sure to leave everyone a flyer or sticker with your website and social media profiles' URLs, or add them to a messaging group and tell them that you are going to run a new giveaway with more prizes at a different location. Set a date for the reveal and ask them to spread the word in the meanwhile. The possibilities are endless!

Chapter 16: Optimizing Your Viral Marketing Campaigns

You can expect your viral marketing campaigns to go on forever. In fact, viral marketing campaigns are all about maintaining momentum until their capacity for replication and outreach are depleted. Here are the best ways to keep your viral campaigns relevant long after the thrill is gone!

Make Your Content Blog-Worthy

Bloggers all around the internet are always on the hunt for blog-worthy content, and their efforts are coincidentally, a great opportunity to increase your reach while your campaigns are going viral AND after your campaigns have gone viral for two reasons.

One because a well-planned viral campaign will always be worth talking about no matter how much time has passed since it went live, and secondly because it gives bloggers something to post about on their blogs.

This will not only help you to further seed and spread your viral campaigns, but also to build back links to your content, which will in turn increase your traffic, open up new lead-capturing sources and pave the way for new referral conversions and sales.

Now, the first step into maintaining your content blog worthy is to always keep it fresh and visually pleasing. Keeping it fresh means to update it with notes and references, and keeping it visually pleasing means to keep the content visually consistent with the rest of your site.

After a certain time, you will want to add the logos of some of the most relevant blogs that have shared, covered or featured your viral campaigns to your content, as that will help you to further build brand relevance and recall.

Include The Right Share Buttons

It is no secret that the more ways you give your audience to share your content, the more it will be shared, and share buttons are great for encouraging social sharing, but you have to know what share buttons are right for your campaign.

Not only that, but you will need to stay vigilant and learn where your content is being shared and what audiences are being exposed to your viral campaigns in order to add or eliminate certain share buttons on your campaigns.

For example, if you see that your viral campaigns are reaching the 20-somethings demographic of graphic designers and gamers, add share buttons for sites such as YouTube, Tumblr, Twitter and StumbleUpon. If they're reaching 40 year old book lovers, add share buttons to Facebook. If they're reaching female gym lovers in their 30s, add share buttons for Instagram and Pinterest.

Use Customized Hashtags

The idea behind viral marketing is to make sharing your content an effortless task, and customized hashtags are a great way to expand brand awareness when going viral. Universal hashtags are of course important, but unless they're about something with evergreen potential such as the "#giveaway" hashtag, they will only get you as far as their trending power lasts.

Now, when you create custom hashtags for business, the idea is to create a hashtag with the right combination of keywords in order to make it persist over time.

Leverage Middle-Of-Content Calls-To-Action

Make sure to update your lead funnel offerings in your viral content after launch by including updated versions of your optin-forms, newsletter signups, affiliate links and free trial "CTAs" at the middle of your viral content to retain new visitors.

Use Reddit To Build Links

Let's get this out of the way first: going viral on reddit is not easy. However, having an engaged reddit community can help you wonders thanks to the way the reddit algorithm works.

The first method is by creating a subreddit for your brand where you can make your viral stories more visible. There you can use Reddit's social button to make it easier for users on the platform to share and upvote your content.

The second method is by using Reddit's own sponsored link and self-serving advertising options. Both methods are guaranteed to give you a permanent source of referral traffic coming from your viral campaigns no matter how much time has passed since launch!

Access my exclusive Viral Marketing Video Training 2018 at viral.cundell.com/upgrade!

Viral Marketing Made Easy 2018

Section 4

Additional Tips to consider

Access my exclusive Viral Marketing Video Training 2018 at viral.cundell.com/upgrade!

Chapter 17: Do's and Don'ts

Do's

Create With Emotions In Mind

Marketing content goes viral when it hits an emotional chord in your audience, so always make sure to create unique, humorous, positive content regardless of whether you will be sending your marketing message through written word or visually rich media.

Make It Easy To Share Your Content

Viral marketing is all about allowing your audience to spread your content through viral sharing, which means that you'll have to make sharing as easy as possible by including social media buttons, embed codes, and forwarding calls-to-action in every placement that your content is posted.

Create A Viral Marketing Plan

Marketing campaigns rarely go "viral" in the way that random viral content does. Your viral marketing campaigns have to be well-planned, they have to make sense at a brand-activity level, and they have to generate a business-centric result such as creating buzz, building brand awareness or driving sales.

Follow Up

Don't be a one-hit wonder! Always follow up your viral marketing campaigns after they end to keep engagement alive by posting follow up videos, blog posts, behind-the-scenes content or sequel campaigns!

Do Something Unexpected

One way to spark curiosity and make content go viral is by simply adding an element of surprise on your marketing materials, such as creating quirky video thumbnails or thought-provoking headlines.

Know Who You Are Targeting At First

Make sure to only reach qualified targets when you first launch your viral campaign, as only targets that are potentially interested in your content will start to virally share it with their like-minded contacts; It will spread like crazy everywhere else from then on!

Focus On Storytelling

Your marketing content and message has to follow a story with punch in order to encourage people to pass it onto others. Remember, even the simplest of memes have been about telling some sort of story.

Tease Your Audience

Spark your audience's curiosity by not telling them exactly what your campaigns are all about, teasing them with small tidbits of your content in titles or thumbnails, leaving them hanging and eager to click and share!

Be Prepared For Unexpected Outcomes!

Sometimes, viral campaigns don't go the way they were intended to; Sometimes they turn out to be 100 times more successful than their creators expected, and sometimes they end up getting overwhelmingly negative responses, so be prepared!

Participate

Viral marketing campaigns are a great opportunity to step in and join the conversation by interacting with your base audience!

Don'ts

Don't Go Negative

Negative or vulgar content often goes viral just because they trigger curiosity tied to negative emotions such as anger or sadness, which isn't good for a brand or a business, so don't get negative just for the sake of being controversial!

Don't Auto Post

Make sure to not post the same message on every channel and instead take the time to create a well-timed editorial to best fit every one of your target platforms!

Don't Blast People On Social Media

You don't have to post incessantly on social media to go viral; In fact, that will only help you to annoy people. Instead, let people be the ones to post incessantly for you; Your message will get the attention it deserves, and your campaigns will go viral beyond your intended reach!

Don't Put Your Brand At The Forefront

Don't focus your viral campaigns on your brand. Simply focus on creating emotionally charged content that is sponsored by your brand and that is consistent with what it offers; This will allow you to generate levels of brand recall that not even paid advertising can match!

Don't Restrict Access

Don't tease your target audience with an awesome headline or image to then send them to a pay wall or registration page. That will only cause most people to move on to something else!

Don't Click-Bait

Don't create misleading titles or images in the hopes of getting more attention and clicks, as that will only kill your brand's reputation before you have a chance to go viral.

Don't Overproduce

Your marketing material doesn't need to look overtly professional in order to go viral. In fact, the opposite works best because people are more attracted to and are more likely to share authenticity.

Don't Tell People How To React

The emotions created by your viral campaigns have to be consistent with your message, so don't try to tell people what type of reaction you are looking to elicit, or you will risk losing the viral punch!

Don't Argue With Your Audience

Some people will react negatively to your viral content, and that's ok. The idea behind viral marketing is to spread your message by encouraging sharing and sparking brand-centric conversations. So don't respond to harsh comments yourself, as that will only give your brand a bad rep!

Don't be misleading

Creating a viral marketing campaign focused on a fictional premise or character is not bad as long as you are transparent about it from the onset, or if you gradually unravel the truth, but don't try to keep a marketing lie buried because it will backfire!

Chapter 18: Premium tools and Services to consider

Viralsweep

"Viralsweep" is an all-in-one viral marketing platform that will provide you with all the right tools to achieve the most important marketing goals right from the onset because it will allow you to rapidly grow your lists through viral sweepstakes and contests, to build beautiful and embeddable email forms, to hire influencers through the Viralsweep platform to promote your campaigns for you, and to partner with other brands that can help you viralize your content further!

Ruzzit.com

"Ruzzit" is a site that aggregates viral content in video, image, and text formats, and is one of our top most recommendations for when you need to look for inspiration to create your next viral campaigns, or simply when you need your brand to stay top-of-mind through trending updates!

Viral Seeding

"Viral Seeding" is a premium platform that specializes in viral content seeding as well as an influencer marketing agency that is equipped to create results-oriented viral campaigns that are tailored to your most immediate business needs.

Prefinery

"Prefinery" is a viral marketing tool that will allow you to integrate engaging sign-up forms everywhere. Now, these are not your normal, run-of-mill sign-up forms, because they capture email addresses to build waiting lists that accelerate viral growth through drip email campaigns that encourage viral sharing once your campaigns launch!

Viral Loops

"Viral Loops" is a revolutionary template-based viral marketing solution for modern marketers. It will allow you to run referral-based activities such as viral content campaigns and giveaways, all through a single plug-and-play platform. All that you will have to do is to select the template that best suits your business and your marketing goals!

Websta

Using hashtags is a great way of giving your content some extra attention and discoverability potential. "Websta" is a website that will help you to find the most widely used hashtags on any given day so you don't have to comb for them on social media!

Norbert

Email is still a great way of spreading viral marketing campaigns, and the more contacts that are able to forward a viral message, the better. "Norbert" is an online-based tool that can help you to find qualified email leads based on data such as names, companies, and corporate websites, leads that you can leverage later on as part of a network of contacts that can help you to take your viral content out there!

Detective

"Detective" is an awesome tool that will allow you to know your email contacts better after capturing them. It helps you by prospecting your leads on autopilot, so you are better prepared to serve them the most appropriate content before launching your next viral campaigns!

Buffergram

"Buffergram" is a professional social media automation, scheduling and publishing service that can help you to better manage your viral marketing campaigns in one of the most viral-friendly social environments available: Instagram!

Viral Shot

"Viral Shot" is an online marketing agency that specializes in viral marketing and social media marketing, and their experts will be able to generate campaigns that are tailored to your needs once you are ready to go viral, spread awareness, generate massive traffic, lots of leads and social media interactions!

Chapter 19: Shocking Case Studies

Google Android

Google Android, or most commonly known simply as "Android", is Google's own mobile operating system, which is currently the most widely used by smartphone manufacturers because of its open source nature.

Objective: Google's objective was to further raise awareness about its Android brand by creating a piece of highly-shareable content that could work as an extension of its brand message.

Strategy: Google produced a short spot featuring unconventional pairs of animals interacting. Aptly titled "Friends Furever", the video was intended to elicit strong emotional responses linked to feelings of friendship to expand the brand's "be together, not the same" message.

Results: The emotional factor in play combined with the overall "cuteness" of the video has made it the single most shared video ad of all time, with over 6.4 million shares across all channels.

Loctite

"Loctite" is the name of a popular glue maker from Germany. It produces adhesives, sealants, and a wide variety of surface treatments that are used by industries and hobbyists all around the world.

Objective: The company's objective was to reach the new generation of digital savvy youngsters that might have not heard of the brand or used its products up to that point.

Strategy: Loctite spent its entire annual marketing budget on a bet when they commissioned a marketing agency to produce a super bowl commercial for the brand. This agency created a funny video ad featuring everyday people using Loctite's products to fix stuff and doing the "Loctite Dance" at the end of the ad.

Results: The goofiness and positive feelings evoked by the video paid off big time, with over a million impressions on YouTube alone, increased brand recall among the target audience and increased sales!

McDonalds

McDonalds is one of the world's most popular fast food chains. In fact, it is the second largest fast food restaurant chain based on the number of locations around the world.

Objective: McDonalds wanted to recapture the attention of younger members of its target audience who were heading to other fast food restaurants, dropping McDonalds market share as low as 12.9 percent.

Strategy: The company crafted a video ad to promote its "Pay With Lovin" campaign, which encouraged people to go to any McDonalds location for the chance to pay for their meals with selfies, hugs, smiles, and the such.

Results: The campaign was an instant viral hit, generating over 8 million views on YouTube within the first 4 days of going live! It was such a viral success that customers and employees started uploading their own videos of them paying with friendly gestures!

Old Spice

"Old Spice" is a very popular American brand of grooming products for males.

Objective: The brand wanted to change its image to appeal to males aged 17 to 35 years old, who favorited brands such as AXE and DOVE.

Strategy: The company created a character that came to be known simply as the "Old Spice Guy", and who was featured in a series of ads that later invited consumers to submit their own comments and sections on the company's social media channels.

Results: The "Old Spice Guy" campaign generated viral levels of response from the get go, with the interactive questions ad generating 5.9 million views on YouTube in a single day and a 125% increase in sales!

Whiskas

"Whiskas" is a worldwide popular brand of cat food which products can be easily recognized by their purple-colored packaging and stylized logo.

Objective: The brand wanted to expand its influence among targets in the "kitten lover" audience and to increase awareness about its wide selection of products.

Strategy: Whiskas partnered with Google and a media agency to create a series of educational videos aimed at cat lovers to be promoted on a YouTube channel which they aptly named "Kitten Kollege".

Results: The "Kitten Kollege" campaign totally exceeded the company's expectations. It generated more than 39 million views as well as a 47% lift in ad recall. Also, it drove positive changes in people's perception of Whiskas as a brand according to some people involved in the campaign.

DC Shoes

"DC Shoes" is an American sports wear brand made popular by its skateboarding shoes. It also manufactures apparel, bags, accessories, hats, shirts, and posters.

Objective: The brand wanted to reinvigorate its brand image and message by leveraging brand loyalty.

Strategy: The brand partnered with Biker Robbie Maddison to record a video of him riding waves on his bike in Tahiti. The goal of the video was to give its fan base the chance to share a campaign that went way out of the ordinary while maintaining an authentic, organic flair.

Results: The "Pipe Dream" campaign was a massive viral success. It garnered over 9million views on YouTube within 48 hours, and it promoted enhanced brand awareness for DC Shoes.

Chris Gimmer

Chris Gimmer is an online entrepreneur, best known as the founder of the Bootstrapbay.com website, a marketplace for themes built the bootstrap framework.

Objective: Chris' objective was to generate awareness about his newly founded website among the bootstrap theme niche audience.

Strategy: Chris used the most popular type of content in his niche to create an improved version of it in one of his site's blog posts to promote sites that offered free stock photos. He then promoted his blog post on reddit and Stumbleupon.

Results: Chris' piece was a viral success right from the start, as it generated over 17,000 visitors to his website in a single day, and has been shared over 240,000 times on social media, which are big numbers for a new, niche-centric website!

Listerine

Listerine is an oral care products brand mostly known for its "Cool Mint" line of mouthwashes.

Objective: Listerine wanted to tackle the young Hong Kong based audience by encouraging the use of Listerine mouthwash before important moments as a way to increase brand awareness and sales in the region.

Strategy: The brand created a viral video ad campaign where they showed a brand ambassador practicing his romantic-advance gestures with a lady while emphasizing the importance of good oral health. The audience was encouraged to participate in the campaign by sharing their own versions of the video ad.

Results: The viral video ad generated over 100,000 views within the first 100 hours of the campaign's launch, as well as over 2,000 branded experiences and product sample requests.

Dollar Shave Club

The "Dollar Shave Club" is a California-based company that delivers personal grooming products to its customers by mail on a subscription basis.

Objective: The company needed to go from start-up to profitable business as fast as possible under a small budget.

Strategy: The brand commissioned a video ad campaign charged with humor, sarcasm and wit to promote their grooming products. They kept the message simple, straight, and highly targeted.

Results: It only took one video for the company to go insanely viral. Their website crashed in the first hour of the campaign's release due to the amount of traffic. Its YouTube channel gained over 12,000 subscribers within 48 hours, and the company rapidly grew to 900,000 subscriptions and 60$ million in sales, all from one viral video ad campaign!

Visa

"Visa" is a large multinational corporation that offers financial services across the world.

Objective: Visa's objective was to influence decision makers in banks, merchant businesses and governments in the Asian region through relevant content.

Strategy: Visa created a Tumblr Newsroom section where it released engaging video content to discuss serious topics such as innovation in economics. It then reached out to its audience by leveraging content searches on premium publisher sites.

Results: This strategy has earned Visa ongoing viral success, with a 270% increase in click-through rates, a 95% increase in new daily visitors, and a steady 75,000 engaged users daily!

Chapter 20: Frequently Asked Questions

Why Is Viral Marketing Labeled As, Well, "Viral"?

The simplest explanation as to why viral marketing is called "viral" is because it spreads a message that self-replicates like a virus. The term precedes digital marketing and was first coined in the 1990s.

Once viral marketing reached digital distribution it started to be described as an idea that spreads like a computer virus, with targets of a campaign getting "infected" and spreading the message.

Should All Online Marketing Campaigns Strive To Go Viral?

Not all brands, products or services will benefit from a viral marketing campaign. Indeed, there have been cases of viral marketing campaigns backfiring.

Ask yourself: Will my offer benefit from being tied to a viral message that might cause my targets to only recall the campaign and not my brand?

Is The Word "Viral" A Way To Describe Any Successful Online Marketing Campaign?

People tend to confuse being "viral" with being wildly successful, but there is a series of subtle differences in between. First and foremost, viral campaigns are planned in advance with the intention of going viral through a very specific message, whereas most marketing campaigns are simply set up to reach a very specific niche subset of a target audience.

What that means is that viral campaigns are designed to reach as many people as possible, wherever possible and at the fastest rate possible, while common marketing campaigns are designed to reach as many people as possible within a qualified target audience.

The idea behind the viral approach is mainly to create massive awareness about a brand or product in order to drive additional marketing objectives depending on people's response to the campaign. On the other hand, the basic online marketing approach pursues a set of very specific marketing objectives from the very beginning, such as driving sales or creating engagement.

Secondly, viral marketing campaigns are fueled by viral sharing, which is encouraged by delivering emotionally charged or highly entertaining content with high probabilities of being shared, while basic marketing campaigns are driven by delivering relevant content through organic marketing channels and paid advertising.

Lastly, viral campaigns are not necessarily considered successful when they don't help a business to achieve profitable marketing objectives beyond the initial short-term impact of going viral.

What's The Most Common Shortcoming You Can Find In Failed Viral Marketing Campaigns?

The biggest mistake that you will see one failed campaign after another is in not being transparent about what the campaign is all about, and the most common form of this is in disguising an advertising campaign as a viral marketing campaign.
The best way to spot a failing campaign is by learning to identify obvious product placement in what otherwise looks like organically produced online material.

Is Viral Marketing The Same As Guerrilla Marketing?

No, and in fact, they're pretty different forms of marketing, yet people tend to confuse both terms because both are designed to generate quick and massive user responses. As we all know by now, viral marketing is simply a way of delivering a highly shareable form of marketing message to be spread by the target audience.

On the other hand, guerrilla marketing is an unconventional marketing method that allows marketers to break common marketing rules such as positioning marketing campaign content on a single placement for an extended period of time, as the idea behind guerrilla marketing is to create a huge impact with unexpected activities.

Flash-mobs and advertising in front of a competitor's business location are examples of guerrilla marketing.

What Should You Consider Before Launching A Viral Marketing Campaign?

First, you have to consider that viral marketing campaigns are seeded, not launched. Seeding a viral marketing campaign means that you have to investigate where is the best place to start promoting your campaign. In other words, you have to look where your audience hangs online so you can "seed" your campaign in there.

Secondly, you have to consider how you are going to measure the success of your campaign after it reaches peak sharing to decide on your next move, considering all the possible outcomes.

Should You Have To Offer A Reward To Incentivize Viral Sharing?

Not necessarily. Unless you are promoting a sweepstake to increase your chances of going viral with a piece of affiliate content, the only reward that your audience will crave is the personal satisfaction of seeing something that they shared being shared tenfold by others.

The reward here is the sensation of making a piece of content to go beyond their own reach, which will give your targets a sense of accomplishment, as it makes them feel like it went viral because they liked it.

What's The Best Way To Share A Viral Marketing Campaign?

It totally depends on the format of the campaign. Is it a very short video or image? Share it on social media. Is it a piece of engaging text? Share it on instant messaging apps. Is it a long form video? Share it on video sharing platforms.

And what if it is a procedurally generated message accompanied by a long-form video that leads to a gated piece of content that you want to go viral by adding an air of exclusivity to it just like Hotmail and Gmail did in their earlier days? Then share it through email!

Seriously? Can Viral Marketing Work With Private, Gated Content?

When done right, yes, it totally can, but mostly because it will drive the opposite effect of staying private. You see, viral marketing campaigns can start "private" by offering a select group of targets a reward through email or social media messaging, all the while sending it off "by accident" to recipients that weren't intended to receive word of such a campaign or reward.

These types of campaigns get viral soon because the unintended recipients start spreading the word about the seemingly secret campaign until it gets public!

What Prevents A Viral Marketing Campaign From Achieving Worldwide Reach?

Cultural differences and language barriers are the most prevalent causes preventing viral campaigns from reaching a worldwide audience. In order for a viral campaign to achieve worldwide success it needs to include elements that people around the world can easily identify with.

Viral marketing campaigns that use slang or specific symbology will get as far as people are able to recognize the campaign's elements!

Conclusion:

We're thrilled that you have chosen to take advantage of our Training Guide, and we wish you amazing success.

And in order to take your Viral Marketing Efforts even farther, we invite you to get the most out of it by firstly downloading our free complementary Cheat Sheet, Resource Report and Mindmap at viral.cundell.com/bonus where you'll also be invited to get access to our Step by Step Video Training, which you can also access from viral.cundell.com/upgrade .

Thanks so much for the time you have dedicated to learning how to get the most advantages from Viral Marketing.

Viral Marketing have come to stay in the market forever.

To Your Success,

Paul Cundell

Top Resources

Videos
https://www.youtube.com/watch?v=IcN9Uv9JLYE
https://www.youtube.com/watch?v=D0QJgx_C4rc

Tools & Services
https://untorch.com/
http://radurls.com/

Training Courses
https://www.educba.com/course/viral-marketing/
https://es.coursera.org/learn/wharton-contagious-viral-marketing

Blogs
https://neilpatel.com/blog/how-to-create-viral-content-that-will-drive-2500-visitors-per-day/
https://www.ikf.co.in/blog/nine-best-viral-marketing-tactics/

Forums
https://www.warriorforum.com/tags/viral%20marketing.html
https://www.blackhatworld.com/tags/viral-marketing/

Affiliate Programs
https://affiliate-program.amazon.com
https://www.clickbank.com/

Webinars
https://www.youtube.com/watch?v=g0CsEJx7czw
https://www.youtube.com/watch?v=50bYwYnu06U

Infographics
https://i0.wp.com/socialmediaexp.wpengine.com/wp-content/uploads/2013/06/5-key-elements-of-viral-content-v2.png?resize=600%2C1610
https://i.pinimg.com/originals/2d/79/3c/2d793c7634161275449e18b192effb94.jpg

Case Studies
http://www.frac.tl/portfolio-item/viral-marketing-case-study/
https://backlinko.com/viral-marketing

Facts
https://www.wordstream.com/blog/ws/2017/03/08/video-marketing-statistics
http://www.frac.tl/content-marketing-statistics/

Access my exclusive Viral Marketing Video Training 2018 at viral.cundell.com/upgrade!

Made in the USA
Middletown, DE
13 July 2019